NOTHINGMAS DAY

ALLISON & BUSBY LTD
LONDON · NEW YORK

First published in Great Britain in 1984 by
Allison & Busby Ltd
6a Noel Street
London W1V 3RB
and distributed in the USA by
Schocken Books Inc.,
200 Madison Avenue
New York, NY 10016

British Library Cataloguing in Publication Data
Mitchell, Adrian
Nothingmas Day
I. Title II. Lawrence, John
821 914   PR6063·I77

ISBN 0 85031 532 8

Set in Century Old Style by Falcon Graphic Art Ltd, Wallington, Surrey
Design and production by Charmian Allwright
Printed and bound in Great Britain by
Billings and Son Ltd, Worcester

This book is dedicated to:

my astonishing children

the only slightly less astonishing children of my friends

the likewise astonishing children and teachers of Billericay School in Essex,
where I spent two years as Visiting Writer and where I wrote several of
these poems in classrooms when I should have been working

my wife, my friends and my animals

Contents

Acknowledgements

Poems in this book have appeared in *Poems* (Jonathan Cape), *Out Loud* (Writers and Readers Cooperative), *Ride the Nightmare* (Jonathan Cape) and *The Apeman Cometh* (Jonathan Cape).

Stufferation

Lovers lie around in it
Broken glass is found in it
Grass
I like that stuff

Tuna fish get trapped in it
Legs come wrapped in it
Nylon
I like that stuff

Eskimos and tramps chew it
Madame Tussaud gave status to it
Wax
I like that stuff

Elephants get sprayed with it
Scotch is made with it
Water
I like that stuff

Clergy are dumbfounded by it
Bones are surrounded by it
Flesh
I like that stuff

Harps are strung with it
Mattresses are sprung with it
Wire
I like that stuff

Carpenters make cots of it
Undertakers use lots of it

Wood
I like that stuff

Cigarettes are lit by it
Pensioners get happy when they sit by it
Fire
I like that stuff

Dankworth's alto is made of it, most of it,
Scoobdidoo is composed of it
Plastic
I like that stuff

Apemen take it to make them hairier
I ate a ton of it in Bulgaria
Yoghurt
I like that stuff

Man-made fibres and raw materials
Old rolled gold and breakfast cereals
Platinum linoleum
I like that stuff

Skin on my hands
Hair on my head
Toenails on my feet
And linen on the bed

Well I like that stuff
Yes I like that stuff
The earth
Is made of earth
And I like that stuff

Give us a Brake

The runaway train knocked the buffers flat:
"Hey!" said the Stationmaster. "That's enough of that.
I've been forty-two years at this station
And I've never seen such bufferation."

The Woman of Water

There once was a woman of water
Refused a Wizard her hand.
So he took the tears of a statue
And the weight from a grain of sand
And he squeezed the sap from a comet
And the height from a cypress tree
And he drained the dark from midnight
And he charmed the brains from a bee
And he soured the mixture with thunder
And stirred it with ice from hell
And the woman of water drank it down
And she changed into a well.

There once was a woman of water
Who was changed into a well
And the well smiled up at the Wizard
And down down down that old Wizard fell. . . .

I Am Boj

(To be shouted, in the voice of a terrible giant, at children who wake early)

I am Boj
I crackle like the Wig of a Judge

I am Boj
My eyes boil over with Hodge-Podge

I am Boj
Organized Sludge and a Thunder-Wedge

I am Boj
I am a Tower of solid Grudge

I am Boj
The molten Centre, the cutting Edge

I am Boj
from blackest Dudgeon I swing my Bludgeon

I am Boj

Elephant Poems

The Galactic Pachyderm

The elephant stands
    among the stars
He jumps off
    Neptune
bounces off
    Mars
to adventures on
    Venus
while his children
    play
in the diamond jungles
    of the
Milky Way

Tinkling the Ivories

There was an elephant
        called Art Tatum
He played a piano
        whose keys were human teeth

Non-event

If an elephant could meet a whale
their understanding would be huge
and they would love one another for ever

Pride

The elephant
is not proud of being an elephant
So why are we ashamed?

Good Taste

The vilest furniture in this land
is an elephant's foot umbrella stand

Love Poem, Elephant Poem

Elephants are as amazing as love
but love is as amazing as elephants
Love is as amazing as elephants
but elephants are as amazing as love

Elephant Values

Nowhere in the world
is there an elephant bad enough
to make a career in advertising
or play full-back for Leeds United

You Aren't What You Eat

The elephant
who's seldom flustered
despises calming food
like custard
Devouring curry
in a hurry
washed down with
a mug of mustard

Turn Turn Turn

There is a time for considering elephants
There is no time for not considering elephants

The infant elephant speaks:

I got a rusk
stuck on my tusk

The Fox

A fox among the shadows of the town,
Should I surrender to the arms of man?
   On the blank icehills lies in wait
   The fighting cold who has thrown down
   His challenge. I'll not imitate
   The feline compromise. I scan
   With warring eyes the servile fate
Of animals who joined the heated town.

Lean-hearted lions in the concrete zoo
Grow bellies, tendons slacken in pale hide,
   Their breath slows to a dying pace.
   Their keepers love them? Tell me who
   Would cage his love in such a place,
   Where only fish are satisfied?
   The keeper has a huntsman's face.
His grasping love would kill me in the zoo.

A scavenger throughout the snowing wind
I peel the sweet bark from the frozen tree
   Or trap the bird with springing jaws.
   The sun retreats out of my mind.
   How could I give this waking pause
   When death's my sleeping company?
   Mad empty, licking at my sores,
I howl this bitter and unloving wind.

Furious in the savage winter day
The crimson riders hounded me from birth
    Through landscapes built of thorn and stone.
    Though I must be their sudden prey,
    Torn to my terror's skeleton,
    Or go to the forgotten earth;
    I will have hunted too, alone,
I will have wandered in my handsome day.

Four seasons wrestle me, I throw them all
And live to tumble with another year
    In love or battle. I'll not fly
    From mindless elements and fall
    A victim to the keeper's lie.
    The field is mine; but still I fear
    Strong death, my watching enemy,
Though seasons pass and I survive them all.

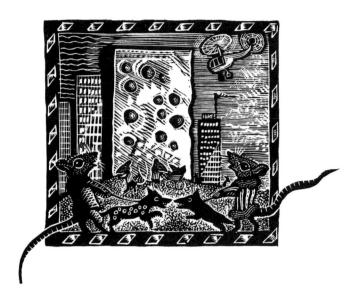

Official Notice

Persons with Dogs or Chimpanzees:
Try to distract their attention, please,
When promenading past the Giant Cheese.

Ode To Dennis The Menace And His Gang

There are Four Seasons of the Beano:

Chocolate Eggs!
                Sandcastle Contest!
                                Fireworks!
and

        Xmas Stocking!

Oh Xmas Stocking! Favourite Season!
When all along the top of the fat word

              BEANO

lies
like a generous layer of icing on the cakes in a box of tuck

        Snow! As in Snowmen!
        Snow! As in Snowballs!

        Snow!
Snow!   Snow!   Snow!
      which falls and drifts in every Reader's dreams

Two-Minute Girl

(In some schools, two minutes before classes start, a Two-Minute Girl or Boy pokes his or her head round the Staffroom door and warns the teachers to Get Ready)

I'm the Two-Minute Girl
I'm about the size of a briefcase
I have bunches done up with barbed wire
And Count Dracula pointy teeth

I'm the Two-Minute Girl
I'm as sweet as syrup pudding on the surface
But I'm as wicked as stinging nettles underneath

Two minutes early or two minutes late
I stick my head round the Staffroom door
And sometimes I whisper like the ghost of a snake
(two minutes) and leave the teachers to snore

Yes I'm the Two-Minute Girl
I'm as cunning as cunning can be
With the driving brain of a diesel train
And the mischieviousness of a flea

Oh I'm the Two-Minute Girl
I love to spread the Two-Minute Blues
Especially when I bellow TWO MINUTES!
And a teacher pours the teapot all over his new suede shoes

Hate Poem

(This was written in a school with the collaboration of about twenty girls and boys. They suggested all the hated items, but as our discussion progressed a small war broke out between the boys and the girls. . . .)

Rounders — it's a girls' game.
Treacle — it's disgusting.
Mushrooms taste of rubber.
Flowers make me sneeze.
Cereal is soggy.
Fish, blood and buses,
Worms, wasps, medicine,
Punks and bees.

I hate spinach,
It's slimy and sloshy.
Sensodyne toothpaste
And Superglue
I hate lizards and Mister B —
(I wouldn't put that in
If I was you).

I hate girls —
When we're trying to play
Football, they play netball
And get in our way.
I hate the smell of dog food,
I hate short hair,
And six boys that's sitting over there.

I hate my sister —
She's too nosey.
I hate to make my brother's
Messy bed every day.
Boys are insane,
Boys are madmen —
I hate the boy who just took
My chair away.

Girls think they're great.
Boy's think they're strong.
You're a lunatic.
You're a lout.
You couldn't fight a bone.
You couldn't fight a flea.
I better stop this verse
Before a fight breaks out.

A Speck Speaks

About ten million years ago
I was a speck of rock in a vast black rock.
My address was:
    Vast Black Rock,
    Near Italy,
    Twelve Metres Under
The Mediterranean Sea.

The other specks and I
Formed an impressive edifice —
Bulbously curving at the base
With rounded caves
And fun tunnels for the fish,
Romantically jagged at the top.

Life, for us specks, was uneventful —
One for all, welded together
In the cool, salty wet.
What more could specks
Expect?

Each year a few of us were lost,
Scrubbed from the edges of the rock
By the washerwoman waters
Which smoothed our base, whittled our cornices
And sharpened our pinnacles.
As the rock slowly shed skin-thin layers
It was my turn to be exposed
Among the packed grit of its surface,
(Near the tip of the fifty-ninth spire
From the end of the eastern outcrop).

One day, it was a Wednesday I remember,
A scampi flicked me off my perch
Near the vast black rock's peak
And I was scurried down
Long corridors of currents
Until a wave caught me in its mouth
And spat me out on —
What?

A drying stretch
Of yellow, white, black, red and transparent specks,
Billions of particles,
Loosely organized in bumps and dips;
Quite unlike the tight hard group
Which I belonged to in the good old rock.
Heat banged down on us all day long.
Us? I turned to the speck next to me,
A lumpish red fellow who'd been washed off a brick.

"I'm new here," I confessed,
"What are we supposed to be?"
He bellowed back —
(But the bellow of a speck
Is less than the whispering of ants) —
"We're grains now, grains of sand,
And this society is called Beach."

"Beach?" I said. "What are we grains supposed to do?"
"Just stray around, lie loose,
Go with the wind, go with the sea
And sink down when you're trodden on."

"Don't know if I can manage that.
Used to belong to Vast Black Rock
And we all stuck together."

"Give Beach a try," said the red grain.
Well, there was no alternative.

Many eras later
I was just beginning to feel
Part of Beach, that slow-drifting,
Slow-shifting, casual community,
When I was shovelled up
With a ton of fellow grains,
Hoisted into a lorry, shaken down a road,
Washed, sifted and poured in a machine
Hotter than the sunshine.

When they poured me out, life had changed again.
My mates and I swam in a molten river
Down into a mould.
White-hot we were, then red, then
Suddenly cold
And we found ourselves merged
Into a tall, circular tower,
Wide at the bottom, narrow at the top
What's more, we'd all turned green as sea-weed.
Transparent green.
We had become — a wine bottle.

In a few flashes of time
We'd been filled with wine,
Stoppered, labelled, bumped to a shop,
Stood in a window, sold, refrigerated,
Drained by English tourists,
Transmogrified into a lampstand,
Smashed by a four-year-old called Tarquin,
Swept up, chucked in the garbage, hauled away,
Dumped and bulldozed into the sea.

Now the underwater years sandpaper away
My shield-shaped fragment of bottle.
So one day I shall be a single grain again,
A single grain of green, transparent glass.

When that day comes
I will transmit a sub-aquatic call
To all green specks of glass
Proposing that we form
A Vast Green Rock of Glass,
Near Italy,
Twelve Metres Under
The Mediterranean Sea.

Should be pretty spectacular
In about ten million years.

All being well.

Awful Medical Poem

If I had a rusty concrete mixer
I would fill it with Murcheson's Cough Elixir.
Doesn't the thought of it make you sick, sir?

eep Sherbet

deep sherbet
in a cardboard
cylinder
printed red
and yellow

used to poke
my liquorice
tube down through
the top and sucked

and when the sherbet
hit the spittle
on my palate —
that's when the fizz began

The Battle-Hymn Of The
Ice-Cream Connoisseur

Mine eyes have seen the glory of
    Pink Fudge Sundaes
I guzzle 'em on Saturdays and slurp on Mondays
I smuggle 'em to Chapel in my Grandma's undies
As my stomach rumbles on.

John Keats Eats His Porridge

It was hot enough to blister
The red paint of his mouth.
But if he let it lie there, glistening,
then clipped segments from the circumference,
it slid down like a soggy bobsleigh.

Grey as November, united as the Kingdom
but the longer he stared into that disc of porridge
the more clearly he traced
under the molten sugar
the outline of each flake of oatmeal.

When the milk made its slow blue-tinted leap
    from jug to bowl
the porridge became an island.
John's spoon vibrated in his hand.
The island became a planet.
He made continents, he made seas.

This is strange porridge.
Eat it all up.

Not A Very Cheerful Song, I'm Afraid

There was a gloomy lady,
With a gloomy duck and a gloomy drake,
And they all three wandered gloomily,
Beside a gloomy lake,
On a gloomy, gloomy, gloomy, gloomy, gloomy, gloomy day.

Now underneath that gloomy lake
The gloomy lady's gone.
But the gloomy duck and the gloomy drake
Swim on and on and on,
On a gloomy, gloomy, gloomy, gloomy, gloomy, gloomy day.

Giving Potatoes

STRONG MAN: Mashed potatoes cannot hurt you, darling
Mashed potatoes mean no harm
I have brought you mashed potatoes
From my mashed potato farm.

LADY: Take away your mashed potatoes
Leave them in the desert to dry
Take away your mashed potatoes —
You look like shepherd's pie.

BRASH MAN: A packet of chips, a packet of chips,
Wrapped in the *Daily Mail*,
Golden and juicy and fried for a week
In the blubber of the Great White Whale.

LADY: Take away your fried potatoes
Use them to clean your ears
You can eat your fried potatoes
With Birds-Eye frozen tears.

OLD MAN: I have borne this baked potato
O'er the Generation Gap,
Pray accept this baked potato
Let me lay it in your heated lap.

LADY: Take away your baked potato
In your fusty musty van
Take away your baked potato
You potato-skinned old man.

FRENCHMAN: She rejected all potatoes
              For a thousand night and days
              Till a Frenchman wooed and won her
              With pommes de terre Lyonnaises.

LADY   Oh my corrugated lover
              So creamy and so brown
              Let us fly across to Lyons
              And lay our tubers down.

40

What's That Down There?

What's that down there?
What's that moving?
What's that moving down in the dark
    of this chilly black maze of a cave?

Is it Sarallo —
The scarlet snake with the seven
Silver heads
And fangs that snap like a murder trap?

    What's that down there?
    What's that moving?
    What's that moving down in the dark
        of this chilly black maze of a cave?

Is it Farranaway —
That back-cracking brute
With a hundred horns
And hoofs that hit like horrible hammers?

    What's that down there?
    What's that moving?
    What's that moving down in the dark
        of this chilly black maze of a cave?

Is it Thilissa —
That slippery wisp of
A whispering ghost of a
Girl who died
In the moistness of mist
Which lies like a shroud on
The underground lake
down in the dark in this chilly black maze of a cave?

A Child Is Singing

A child is singing
And nobody listening
But the child who is singing:

Bulldozers grab the earth and shower it.
   The house is on fire.
Gardeners wet the earth and flower it.
   The house is on fire.
   The houses are on fire.
Fetch the fire engine, the fire engine's on fire.
   We will have to hide in a hole.
   We will burn slow, like coal.
All the people are on fire.

And a child is singing
And nobody listening
But the child who is singing.

Watching You Skating

I see two skates
Blue sliding into silver
Silver gliding into blue

I see two moons
One moon reflected in each of the skates
Carrying you

You zip across the blue and silver pond
I am wonderfully fond
Of the moon and the moon-faced pond and you

Song In Space

When man first flew beyond the sky
He looked back into the world's blue eye.
Man said: What makes your eye so blue?
Earth said: The tears in the ocean do.
Why are the seas so full of tears?
Because I've wept so many thousand years.
Why do you weep as you dance through space?
Because I am the Mother of the Human Race.

Nature Poem

Skylark, what prompts your silver song
To fountain up and down the sky?

Beetles roast
With fleas on toast
And earthworm pie.

Beattie Is Three

At the top of the stairs
I ask for her hand.

 O.K.

She gives it to me.
How her fist fits my palm.
A bunch of consolation.
We take our time
Down the steep carpetway
As I wish silently
That the stairs were endless

Up A Hundred-Mile-High Pine Tree With You

Glabber is my name and round is my shape.
I'm a not-so-scary hairy ape.
With a lantern-eyed cat called Candy Floss,
I live in a brandy barrel lined with moss.

From the top of the Hundred-Mile-High Pine Tree
The Princess Miralana dropped a note to me:
"Rescue me! Rescue me! I can be found
In a pine cone a hundred miles above the ground.
So mount the cloudy branches courageously,
For the Wizard of Worsen has enchanted me."

But as soon as I clutched Branch One with my arm
The whole tree started ringing like a fire alarm
The sky gave a shudder and the earth gave a crack
And a Scarlet Vulture stabbed its claws deep into my back.

I grabbed him round the neck with my amazing tail
And squeezed his Adam's apple till his wings turned pale,
Then my huge left foot knocked his hook-beak flat
And I pulled out his feathers and stuck them in my hat.

Then the Vulture swooped off of me screamin' and a-cursin'
And zoomed off to his master — the Wizard of Worsen.
Oh the Wizard of Worsen donned his magical mac
And he hullabalooed as he launched his attack.

On the Silver-Winged Rhino he charged with a dive
Like an interstellar rocket in hyper-drive.
With my back to the tree-trunk I began to sway.
Then, just as the Rhino was three feet away,
I jumped to the left and I swung right around
And was on the Wizard's shoulders with a rubbery bound.

But the Rhino had cracked the great pine tree in two.
And the Wizard was smashed into magical stew.
And the pine cone fell down. And the Princess stepped out.
And she married my cat — which is why I shout:

Glabber is my name and round is my shape.
I'm a not-so-scary hairy ape.
With a lantern-eyed cat called Candy Floss,
And a lovely Princess, and a Sense of Loss,
I live in a brandy barrel lined with moss.

The Ancestors Of Lancelot Quail, One Heck Of A Hero

My mother was the Beauty
My father was the Beast
I'm Mister Hairy Universe
To say the bloody least

My granny was the mountains
My grandpa was the mud
I was born in a bonfire
With gunpowder blood

Great-Grandpa was the North Pole
Great-Granny the Equator
They may freeze me now
But they'll fry me later

Great-Great-Granny was the Amazon
Great-Great-Grandpa was the Nile
So my head is full of jungles
And rocker crocodiles

Great-great-great-grandpa lives on Pluto
Great-great-great-granny comes from Mars
I was born to desperado
As the outlaw of the stars

And if anyone should ask you
Who made this mighty song
Tell them — Lancelot Quail's
The Wonder of Wales —
But now that poor boy's gone. . . .

The Floating Flautist

I wish I lived in a house in the clouds:
I'd serenade wing-clapping seagull crowds.
My flute would purr and ripple and trill
And angels would perch on my window-sill.

HEIFER STIRK RUNS AMOK

Pursued for four hours in Skipton

Walt Disney could have made a wonderful film of the antics of a six-month old Hereford stirk which led its owner, police officers and staff of the Skipton Auction Mart a merry dance on Tuesday. For nearly five hours they pursued the animal, which had gone mad and ran amok, all over Skipton.

The saga really began on Monday morning when the stirk was taken to Skipton Auction Mart to be sold. It was in the calf ring waiting to have a number stuck on its back when it suddenly became fed-up with the whole proceedings and dashed out into the main yard. About 20 farmers tried to capture it, but it bowled one of them over and then made its way down the beck at the rear of the Auction Mart, through King's Foundry land and along Carleton Road into the grounds of Skipton General Hospital. It then swam across the Leeds and Liverpool Canal and climbed out into a field on the Horse Close estate.

Thinking it had taken fright at missing its mother, the owner, Miss Betty Thornton, of Whinburn Farm, Bradley, took the cow to the field in the hope that it would pacify the young stirk and left the two of them in the field during Monday night.

When they went to collect them on Tuesday the stirk dashed away and again jumped into the canal and swam over a mile to Brewery Lane. It then clambered out and slipped down a deep slope into Eller Beck, waded downstream and into a 50 yard tunnel which runs underneath Broughton Road and Dewhurst's Mill.

It stayed in the tunnel for about half an hour, turned round and made its way upstream, climbed out and made its way into Gargrave Road. With members of the Auction Mart staff and police in pursuit, the stirk weaved its way in and out of traffic on the main road and scattered pedestrians.

CHARGED PURSUERS.

It turned into Woodman Terrace, which is a cul-de-sac, and its capture seemed certain. But the stirk, which had horns, put its head down and charged at its pursuers, who scattered. It then continued up Gargrave Road and ran into the grounds of Skipton Girls' High School and on to the tennis courts. Again its capture seemed certain, but each time anyone went near it the animal charged at them, forcing them to retreat.

Cyril Marshall, the Auction Mart foreman, and two Auction Mart workmen, David and Tommy Harrison, who were assisted by Police Sergeant Michael Clemmett and Police-Constable John O'Neil, made repeated attempts to corner the animal. Miss Betty Thornton drove a Land Rover and armed with a stick, the stirk's mother, on to the tennis courts to get the stirk to walk to its mother. Three times it walked up the ramp into the trailer but when efforts were made to close the tailboard it dashed out again.

Cyril Marshall made unsuccessful attempts to lasso the animal. The two police officers then bravely, in true Mata-dor fashion, faced the animal. Carrying a wooden form in front of him Police-constable O'Neil advanced towards the animal and armed only with a stick, Sergeant Clemmett tried to drive it to the trailer. The sergeant had to sidestep smartly when the stirk charged him and it also chased one of the Auction Mart workmen 50 yards across the tennis courts and he had to dive under some netting to escape its horns.

The action became stalemate, and then suddenly the stirk made another wild dash. It ran from the grounds of the Girls' School down the busy Gargrave Road into the grounds of Ermysted's Grammar School. Efforts to catch it here failed, and then it was off again, down the back of Park Avenue, back down Gargrave Road, Coach Street and Broughton Road, along Carleton New Road to the Burnside Estate.

By this time the chase had gone on well over four hours. The stirk then went into the gardens of a bungalow and at the third attempt a cattle transporter, Mr. Long-thorne, succeeded in securing a noose round its neck and the stirk was put into the trailer to be re-united with its mother.

The Brave Heifer Stirk

(Based on a report from the *Craven Herald and Pioneer* of July 17th, 1970)

It is the thirteenth of July
In nineteen-seventy
Farmers pace Skipton marketplace
Unconscious of their jeopardy.

This heifer stirk in the Auction Mart
Is barely six months old,
But the brain beneath its yellow horns
Intones the words: "I'll not be sold."

The number card is all prepared
On the stirk's back to be stuck,
But the heifer stirk bursts from the ring,
Black mind in spate, bloodstream amok.

A score of farmers try to pass
Hairy white ropes around its neck
But the stirk upends the best of them
Then splatters down the beck.

It swaggers through King's Foundry Land
To Skipton Hospital
Launches itself and swings across
The Leeds and Liverpool Canal.

Now Betty Thornton's trailer brings
The mother of the stirk to graze.
Monday night is an armistice
But the dawn sets the stirk ablaze.

Tuesday: and the stirk marches down
To its safe canal again.
It swims about two thousand yards
To disembark at Brewery Lane.

It slithers down to Eller Beck,
Then stamps downstream until
It stands in the black fifty yards
Of tunnel under Dewhurst's Mill.

For half an hour it drinks the dark,
Then re-emerges, thunderously,
Chased by the staff of the Auction Mart
And Skipton Town Constabulary.

In Gargrave Road it toys with cars
And jellifies the passers-by.
"O save us from this heifer stirk!"
The sad pedestrians cry.

Woodman Terrace becomes its lair. . .
A trap! This is a cul-de-sac!
Wheedlers advance with jailers' smiles
But the prongs of fury drive them back.

On the Girl's High School Tennis Courts
Pound those four havoc-wreaking feet.
Men sidle forward, one head is lowered,
Another charge, another mass retreat.

The foreman, Cyril Marshall, comes
From Skipton Auction Mart,
With Dave and Tommy Harrison,
Brothers no stirk shall ever part.

To stop a further charge is the attempt
Of Police Sergeant Michael Clemmett,
But, even helped by Constable O'Neil,
There is no way the law can stem it.

Now the stirk's mother is brought again
By trailer to the Tennis Court,
But though the stirk thrice mounts the ramp
It turns back with a rousing snort.

O, Marshall with his lasso all awhirl,
He cannot do the trick,
Nor Clemmett with a wooden form,
Nor O'Neil with a stick.

The Force means nothing to a stirk,
Freedom's its only rule.
It shoulders traffic all down Gargrave Road
To reach Ermysted's Grammar School.

Park Avenue, Coach Street, Broughton Road,
It takes at thumping rate,
Then stops beside a bungalow
On the Burnside Estate.

Four hours they've stalked that heifer stirk
While it played fast and loose.
Now Mr Longthorne, of the cattle-truck,
Secures it with his wily noose.

So here's a health to the heifer stirk
And the Skipton steeple-chase,
And may all who love their liberty
Run such a pretty race!

The Set-Square, Square-Set Gunman

(for geometricians and Country and Western fans)

I come from Euclid County, where the savage Cosines ride
And under the Geomma Tree I tunes my old guitar.
My pappy was a Cube who took a Spiral fer his bride
So I wuz born to be rectangular.

Yup. Both my sides is parallel and I'm broader than I'm high,
But have no doubt about my shoot-it-out capacity,
Fer I've got more angles than Isosceles, plus a Pythagorean
    eye
And all the cowpokes call me Oblong Cassidy.

56

Bebe Belinda And Carl Columbus

verses for Laura

There was a girl who threw bananas about
When she couldn't get bananas she threw baseball bats about
When she couldn't get baseball bats she threw big blue
    beehives about
And her name was Bebe, Bebe Belinda

There was a boy who threw cuckoo clocks about
When he couldn't find cuckoo clocks he threw cucumbers about
When he couldn't find cucumbers he went crackers and threw
    christening cakes about
And his name was Carl, Carl Columbus

In Hanover Terrace, that magical place,
Bebe and Carl met, face to red face.
She bust his cuckoo clock with a bunch of bananas.
In a swashbuckling sword fight his cucumber cutlass
Carved her baseball bat to bits.
She bashed him on the bonce with her best blue beehive
But he craftily crowned her with a christening cake.

And they left it to me, old Lizzie Lush
To clean up the street with my scrubbing brush.

BRIGHTON, 1981

Their Voices

(A Discussion About Poetry At The Poetry Festival)

for Beattie

One had a voice like an ancient wooden desk
Initials cut deep all over
And then inked in, black, blue and blue-black.

Two had a voice like a rubbish dump —
Old cabbages tumbling out of a sack.

Three had a voice like a fountain on a mountain
And a holiday stream bounding down the rocks.

Four had a voice like a willow-tree.

Five had a voice like a jack-in-the-box.

But what did they say? What decisions were made?
Dunno. I only listened to the music they played.

CAMBRIDGE POETRY FESTIVAL, 1981

Amazing Mathematical Discovery Rocks Universe.
Essex Man Slightly Hurt.

Nobel Maths Wizards Make Odd Discovery —
Two Plus Two Has Stopped Making Four.

TWO PLUS TWO MAKES FIVE AND A BIT!

Schoolkids Burn Dummies of Einstein and Newton,
Those old dummies, as they chant:
Two Plus Two Makes Five And A Bit!

Their faulty arithmetic finally exposed —
Suspension bridges go haywire!
Skyscrapers sway, fold and collapse into their own cellars!
Cash registers, calculators and computers
Short-circuit themselves in mass suicide.
The Thames fills up with stockbrokers and Vatmen!

Only the average people
Whose maths is so far below average
Go about their normal unbusinesslike business —
Making things without measuring them exactly,
Only pretending to count the change,
Buying Two and Two
And being charged Five And A Bit.

Yorkshire Epitaph

he could run right fast

a ginger-golden hump of fur
but his retractable feet could move over the Yorkshire grass
so we called him after the best runner we could remember
      Zatopec

after a night of frost
found dead in his netted house
legs straight out
a dark stain round his mouth
a globe tear in the corner of one eye
he was buried in the flower bed
        Zatopec, our lone guinea pig

he could run right fast

Lost Love Poem

One day they'll manufacture eggs,
The formula for snowflakes will be clear
And love explained — that's not the day
I think about, the day I marked on my calendar.

Because they appreciate their legs,
Simple creatures will career
Through boundless grass. One day, the day
I think about, the day I marked on my calendar.

In the classroom the boy with ragged fingernails
Flicks a note to the girl whose hair solidifies
All the light there is. The note says:
Some day, when I'm grown up, some day —
It falls between the floorboards. . . .

The Clown Is Dead

Children must learn that fairy tales are lies,
Faces are masks, and peace is out of reach.
I stare into the clown's unwinking eyes
Discovering the child they could not teach.

Though he rode out of childhood cheerfully
He left that forest for the open lands
In fear of other men. He could not see
If they held knives or flowers in their hands.

Seeing the animals, he learnt to speak
Solemnly to them, and at length remove
Their simple terrors; for if he was weak
In anything, it was not in his love.

***

Death came to him when he was young
And he stuck out his scarlet tongue.
He went to death when he was old:
"Take me," he said, "it's turning cold."

The Bearded Lady and the Tattooed Man
Played cards inside his caravan.
We sat around his tousled bed,
Shivered with him till he was dead.

That was a quiet way, to fade,
For him, who loved to sit astride
The high giraffe in the parade,
With blare and bang of brass and hide.

It was a quiet way to fall.
Into the ring he used to come
With a high tragic caterwaul —
And always fell upon his bum.

***

What was the colour of his mind?
It was a prism, casting lights,
Changing, revolving in the wind
Of roaring days and storming nights.

Our elephants of laughter strode
Across his earthy doubletalk.
He goaded them to a stampede
And shot them with a popping cork.

He met tired walkers every day.
They were ill with travelling.
His songs enchanted them to stay:
They learnt to sing.

What's left? A clown of empty cloth,
A crumpled rainbow on the floor
Of a black cupboard. The destroying moth
Nest in the shapeless hat he wore.

What remains with any man?
There is no answer.
In this circus no one can
Dance, but he was a dancer.

He had no children, but I would
Stand as his son, to keep his name
And watch his footsteps take the road
Of prancing beyond praise or blame.

***

The gentle unicorn has gone away.
The dodo, poker-faced and knockabout
Saw that its tail was turning grey,
Ate up the door and waddled out.

In his good time he followed these
Moonstruck and happy monsters. All
His laughter has gone with him, and like these
He is extinct or mythical.

And he is fabulously still;
The greasepaint grin wiped off his face
By lightly sliding hands, until
The naked lips grin in its place.

***

In his hands put an apple from a tree,
Bury him deep so no one can see,
For a dead man's smile tears the whole heart down.
The clown is dead. Long live the clown.

The Blackboard

Five foot by five foot
(The smalls have measured it).
Smooth black surface
(Wiped by a small after every class).
Five different colours of chalk
And a class of twenty-five smalls,
One big.

Does the big break up the chalk
Into twenty-five or twenty-six
And invite the smalls to make
A firework show of colours
Shapes and words
Starting on the blackboard
But soon overflowing
   All over the room
      All over the school
         All over the town
            All over the country
               All over the world?

    No.

The big looks at the textbook
Which was written by a big
And published by a firm of bigs.
The textbook says
The names and dates of Nelson's battles.
So the big writes, in white,
Upon the black of the blackboard,
The names and dates of Nelson's battles.
The smalls copy into their books
The names and dates of Nelson's battles.

    Nelson was a big
Who died fighting for freedom or something.

65

Dumb Insolence

I'm big for ten years old
Maybe that's why they get at me

Teachers, parents, cops
Always getting at me

When they get at me

I don't hit em
They can do you for that

I don't swear at em
They can do you for that

I stick my hands in my pockets
And stare at them

And while I stare at them
I think about sick

They call it dumb insolence

They don't like it
But they can't do you for it

My Last Nature Walk

I strode among the clumihacken
Where scrubble nudges to the barfter
Till I whumped into, hidden in the bracken,
A groolted after-laughter-rafter.

(For milty Wah-Zohs do guffaw
Upon a laughter-rafter perch.
But after laughter they balore
Unto a second beam to gurch.)

Yet here was but one gollamonce!
I glumped upon the after-laughter-rafter.
Where was its other-brother? Oh! My bonce!
The Wah-Zohs blammed it with a laughter-rafter.

Moral: Never gamble on a bramble ramble.

GLOSSARY:

clumihacken — the old stalks of wild Brussels sprouts
scrubble – unusually tall moss, often scuffed
the barfter — the height at which low clouds cruise
to whump — to bump into, winding oneself in the process
groolted — cunningly engraved with the portraits of little-known and famous barbers
milty — clean but mean-minded
Wah-Zohs — French birds, sometimes spelt Oiseaux
to balore — to hover fatly downwards
to gurch — to recover from cheerfulness
gollamonce — a thing that is sought for desperately, although there is no good reason
　　　　　　　for finding it.
to glump — to glump
to blam — to shonk on the cloddle

Horrible Everyday Incident
In Horrible Sperlunga

I'm the eight-headed spider of the suburbs of Sperlunga
And all my hatred is reserved for the wicked spider-monger
For he hunts me with metallic flies whose wings bear cruel
   points
And he longs to slice my body into spider steaks and joints

One day I went out strolling on my 64 braw legs
I only paused awhile to lay 500,000 eggs
For I was overflowing with a terrible fanged hunger
To lunch upon the marbled heart of the wicked spider-monger

I saw him in his murder shop a-checking of his till
And thought: You'd do much better to be making out your will
I knew he longed to hang my heads high on his grisly wall
And flaunt his wife in spider-skin at the Spider-mongers' Ball

I watched him pass the Wishing Tree and pass the Crystal
   Sphinx
I watched him pass the Plasma Bar where the Lone Vampire
   drinks
I watched him pass Balloon Lagoon where purple icebergs float
But I caught him by the Coward's Gate and rubbished out his
   throat

She was standing in the shadows with the great eight-bladed
   knife
And now my heads are severed by the spider-monger's wife
Yet my eight mouths died guffawing as they were hacked apart
Half a million eggs are hatching in my white web's woven
   heart. . . .

To My Dog

This gentle beast
This golden beast
laid her long chin
along my wrist

and my wrist
is branded
with her love
and trust

and the salt of my cheek
is hers to lick
so long as I
or she shall last

A Poem For Dogs

(I know plenty of poems about dogs but this is the only one
I ever wrote for a dog, a golden retriever called Polly.
She liked to listen to it while her chest was being tickled.
Try it on a dog you love, changing the name of course, and
reciting over and over in a gentle, deep voice.
You will find that most dogs enjoy this game, especially
after supper).

Good Polly
Good dog.
Good Polly,
Good dog.

A Valentine Poem For Cathy Pompe's Kids
At St Paul's Primary School, Cambridge
(who were about 6-7 years old)

The night is a dark blue balloon
The day is a golden balloon
The moon longs to cuddle the sun
The sun longs to cuddle the moon

A Game To Play With Babies

Ring the bell — ding ding
Press the buzzer — bzzzzzz
Knock at the door — knock knock
And walk in — oh, no thank you!

(The way to play. Ring the bell — pull the earlobe.
Press the buzzer — press the tip of the nose.
Knock at the door — tap the forehead.
And walk in — put your little finger in mouth and withdraw it
        quickly before you're bitten saying, "Oh, no thank you!"
It's best to demonstrate all these movements and words
on yourself a few times until the baby has got the idea.
Then you try the baby's earlobe, nose, forehead and mouth,
But very gently. Be careful with the fourth move — some
babies have tiger teeth. You will find that most babies
enjoy this game, especially after the twentieth repetition.)

Pause

I was just about to say to my daughter:
Look what beautiful eyes that horse has.
When I suddenly stopped and thought:
Maybe horses aren't supposed to have eyes like that.

Musical

Musical rain clouds begin to play
Musical lunatics sway round the corner
Musical girls slide down the hay
Music visits the charcoal-burner

School Dinners

Lumpy custard and liver — ugh!
I hate school dinners and I'll tell you why.
There's dog food with peas in, there's Secret Stew,
And a cheese and bacon thing that we call Sick Pie.

Revenge

The elephant knocked the ground with a stick,
He knocked it slow, he knocked it quick.
He knocked it till his trunk turned black —
Then the ground turned round and knocked him back.

Beattie's Beliefs

God made the world
God made ballet
God made everything

        except fireworks

Nothingmas Day

No it wasn't.

It was Nothingmas Eve and all the children in Notown were not
tingling with excitement as they lay unawake in their heaps.
D
   o
      w
         n
           s
             t
               a
              i
                r
                  s their parents were busily not placing the last
crackermugs, glimmerslips and sweetlumps on the Nothingmas
Tree.

Hey! But what was that invisible trail of chummy sparks or
vaulting stars across the sky
        Father Nothingmas — drawn by 18 or 21
        rainmaidens!
        Father Nothingmas — his sackbut bulging with air!
        Father Nothingmas — was not on his way!
(From the streets of the snowless town came the quiet of
unsung carols and the merry silence of the steeple bell.)

Next morning the children did not fountain out of bed with cries
of WHOOPERATION! They picked up their Nothingmas
Stockings and with traditional quiperamas such as: "Look what
I haven't got! It's just what I didn't want!" pulled their stockings
on their ordinary legs.

For breakfast they ate — breakfast.

After woods they all avoided the Nothingmas Tree, where
Daddy, his face failing to beam like a leaky torch, was not
distributing gemgames, sodaguns, golly-trolleys, jars of
humdrums and packets of slubberated croakers.

Off, off, off went the children to school, soaking each other with
no howls of "Merry Nothingmas and a Happy No Year!", and
not pulping each other with no-balls.

At school Miss Whatnot taught them how to write No Thank
You Letters.

Home they burrowed for Nothingmas Dinner.
The table was not groaning under all manner of
       NO TURKEY
       NO SPICED HAM
       NO SPROUTS
       NO CRANBERRY JELLYSAUCE
       NO NOT NOWT
There was not one (1) shoot of glee as the Nothingmas
Pudding, unlit, was not brought in. Mince pies were not
available, nor was there any demand for them.

Then, as another Nothingmas clobbered to a close, they all
haggled off to bed where they slept happily never after.

    and that is not the end of the story. . . . . . .